the shadow sonnets

the shadow sonnets

richard sommer

NUAGE
EDITIONS

Cover design by Seth Levinson.
Book design and typesetting by Karen Haughian.
Published with the assistance of The Canada Council.
Printed and bound in Canada by Hignell Printing Ltd.

Dépôt légal, Bibliothèque nationale du Québec and the National Library of Canada.

Canadian Cataloguing in Publication Data

Sommer, Richard
The shadow sonnets

Poems.
ISBN 0-921833-17-2

1. Sonnets, Canadian (English). I. Title.

PS8587. O44S43 1992 C811 '. 54 C92-090707-5
PR9199. 3 . S65S43 1991

NuAge Editions, P.O. Box 8, Station E, Montreal, Quebec, H2T 3A5

For my mother, Ida Jerome,
and my wife, Vicki Tansey,
whose intelligent and nurturing energies
link me to those who have gone before
and to those who follow.

foreword

Why sonnets? I just wanted, of course, to see if I could do it, know what it felt like to do sonnets, many of them together, really to swim in sonnetry. Then too, most sonnets to date have been written and spoken or sung by men, mostly to women. By and large it's been a man's form, instrument of seduction, pleading, anger, love, relatedness or distancing, by Milton separated from the subject of our relationship with women, but never completely drawn into the myth of male self-sufficiency. In fact, the sonnet is visibly a place where that myth breaks down, if I read my Petrarch and Shakespeare and Berryman right. Any direction I read, it's the same. The sonnet often betrays, only sometimes acknowledging it, how much we need women, their intuition and vision, no matter how women may decide the complementary question of whether and how much they need us. Perhaps it's this breakdown that has interested me and of which I have relatively gently and generally been in favour, and around and through which I have written these sonnets.

I have wanted to see this traditional and patriarchal instrument of sexist adoration, this verbal pedestal, transformed into a means not just to express power assertions and needs, not just to record the difficulties and failures, nor to gloss them over, but to honour the human relationship in and through its difficulty, its wonder and necessity.

Well, then, why *shadow* sonnets? Among the reasons, first, the form. They aren't strictly sonnets at all, but approximate sonnets, following shadows of the form, their rhymes often proximate rather identical sounds, their metre a play across the defining rules of iambic pentameter rather than in conformity to them. The music I have wanted of them is of near likeness, degrees of similarity, not of exact identity. Usually we hear conventional rhyme as a series of binary off/on states—either it rhymes or it doesn't. What I want listeners to hear are near approaches, whole ranges and degrees of rhyme and conformity to metre. I have, however, usually kept to the simple end-rhyme scheme of Shakespeare—modified with *In Memoriam* quatrains—and to the traditional fourteen lines.

Then too, the shadow sonnets are shadows of the spirit of the sonnet, of its everpresent thread of argument, its dense and gnarled sense of intimate conversation, its erotic unrest, its terrible desire for someone and something unpossessed and not to be possessed. In this, they are shadows of the masters, the poets who have gone before and suffered relationship and who shaped it into the form I have followed. I admire some, though I love Philip Sidney and Hopkins and yes, I admit it, Will Shakespeare, though I have no idea, really, who he was, or is. These and Berryman have most fed me and helped fill these shadows with a certain fertile emptiness which for me, perhaps as a male, illuminates and is real.

In a nearer sense, the poems' shadows are my shadows. They reflect and refract the time of my Saturn's return, a time when all my own secret muddled history of humiliations and hungers and angers and adorations returned to me. It was a time when all the shadow women I have known returned and lent their painful but clarifying presences, forgiving or unforgiving, to a necessary personal dialogue with denied loss and discovery of what remains or is new-found. And much is new-found. Because of this, I hope men as well as women will receive this book and read it: I can't really teach anything to anybody, but if I can give an image and a voice to something that has been silent or silenced in others, I will have accomplished what I set out to do.

I will have shared the delirium of love, the madness, the loss, the finding, the holding to, the steadfastness, and beyond even the love of creatures. Finally, the poems are just broken and awkward shadows of the unconditional love of the earth we all struggle toward, even when we fail to realize it, and must achieve if our world is not to be stripped and burned to a ball of stone, ruled by gangs of ants.

The poems are meant for my grandmothers, my mother, my aunts, my wives, my daughters, lost lovers, old women, women I haven't met yet, at least in this life, and the mountain I've fought for and love and under whose huge and swinging shadow I live. The poems are shadows, outlines of where the light isn't, of my time and place and necessities. It's not easy for me to submit to the forms of the old ones, but this form of the sonnet has carried me into places I could never have dreamed by myself and truths I might never have let myself inhabit, so I feel very grateful.

R. S.
Pinnacle Mountain, Quebec,
September 1992.

1

What's this, another sonnet? Give me a break,
muse, just let me live peaceful for a while—
but now along comes Ray Charles, his one smile,
the outpouring of music he doesn't make,

only finds and brings through his fingers
to me. Nobody knows what he's thinking
or what he's undergone to keep singing
the silly songs he sings, or what of angers

have left him his straight back & blind beaming.
But if I've wondered what love is, still do,
I know I love this old blind man: it's true,
saw in an airport once his being, not seeming,

alone, gently sitting there just waiting
for the next feel of keys, his source of all things.

2

Wild storm last night, but being so doped
on antihistamines & aspirin
I woke up only as in a dream of rain,
dim flashings rumblings not the storm I'd hoped

would come in a black chariot & scour
air & mind & eye nose throat & lungs
& terrify & leave & just let me sing
at height of voice again & as before

be free to say & pattern what's to say
on everything & nothing already spoken
from rotund mouths or cracked, the teeth kicked in
through disease & drugs & love & war & play.

Muse, clean me out & clear me & let me sing
out over this muggy valley, in voice belonging.

3 flying home from arizona

Hearing Miles play Bird in the headphones
I watch a blackhaired girl standing in the aisle
at 30,000 feet, that's near six miles-
& recall the burials of red ochre bones

& think: the ground under our feet is air,
air, air, not even air, nothing:
see you in the next, sweet something,
I suddenly love the tumble of your hair

as you talk to someone I can't see
who means to you whatever he/she means-
& the thinness of your face as you lean
forward to say & hear & say & be

so temporary in the blare of Bird
played by Miles, is written in the stars.

4

Down in the Bread & Puppet Circus Band
surrounded by wild energy of musicians
all tooting their own chaos of precisions
I toot & look over evening on the land.

My flute, another, clarinets & horns,
three saxophones at least, a churning cloud
of sound, drum mutter turned to roar so loud
my bones buzz, yet as I play & slowly turn

at each compass point a different music
enters my ears & rises to my lip.
At center, two Italian girls just sit
in twilight, so beautiful I can't help lose it,

my breath, our melody of the proximate,
everything, to their smiles, open & sentient.

5

So little draws attention to itself
out here in country on a rainy day.
Yesterday was like that, a quiet lake
of small precisely knit events, a wealth

to looking eyes & nothing to purposeful:
leaves each tipping too much waterload
to the one beneath to drink from & to hold,
wet woods & hunched crows & fox curled in hole,

& where was I & what did I manage to do?
An appointment in Granby, a not half-bad poem
not half-good either, & on the way back home
discussed a lumpy tire, bought frozen goo

to mix for juice. Ripe berries in the rain
wet finches got, not I, caught up again.

6

Your fingers wander over & among
objects accidentally tabled in
my memory, papers, a newsclipping,
obituary for some old man once young

you remember (inside my memory)
& ramble on with, as you always did
when I wanted to leave because I was a kid
with a friend waiting & couldn't follow the story,

but look, Grandma: all this poetry
is remembering, a record, a writing after
the fact of now; years later now I'm dafter
& have your stories in my head, now see

no difference, hearing your voice once holding me
in a loving presence, your grandson quick & free.

7

Here I sit curled in a big brown chair
not listening to the rain, but listening to rain
out there, a day of trying to finish things long
ago started or started yesterday or

just dumped here, someone's nest of expectations,
someone's desire, for me? no, for me to do,
something that without me would cause woe,
something athwart whatever stumbling direction

was in mind when I awoke, at dawn,
briefly, out of that metaphor called sleep
but only what it is; my lady's lips
(also no metaphor) drawing me up & on

to love that stood for nothing but itself,
a poem here that stands for nothing I could tell.

8

A moment ago, peeing in a bush
filled with foraging bees, their globe of sunny
humming around my gold-bright arc of running,
me between fear of stings & release-rush,

I thought aha another well-mixed pleasure
bites the flesh of this sudden hush as I
wiggle & put away & try to say
my way out of this fact exerting pressure

on my antennae to the effect that these bees
stopped humming when I put away my dick
& became Richard again, stopped their talk
to me, all of it. I think I'll go back & see

if they start it up again in their world bush,
their sounding & circling around my secret flesh.

9

As I leave the house, Dog bounds over
stone in mouth, wanting me to chase him,
wanting me to run him down, to choose him
to wrestle down & probe with thumb & finger

wet maw, the long white teeth he swings about
as a butcher knives, as a choirboy the censer
& at the middle of this furious fit
the stone itself. I see it is sincere

in being just a stone, any stone
will do for Dog, oh please won't I go for it,
no I'm dressed up to go away, go out
& can't & won't & don't know really when

if ever I'll play his game again, tomorrow
or never (knowing death as he can't, the horror...)

10

Leaves of this butternut answer to the wind
& need the rain & sun & all that stuff
which is the tree's version of love enough.
What's enough? There's never enough in the end.

Now comes the end. Her leaves outside my window
are spotted brown, bud late & fall early.
She's been dying all her life yet barely
endures. Her kind are rare around here now.

And we are getting closer to the end
& the acid in her shadows eats away
at man & tree alike, each in our way
turning brown of leaf, grey of mind

sick at heart & withering in doubt
of this truth in love we try to do without.

11 the pinnacle

Up here in springtime, the prevailing wind
streams hair over cheekbone, brow & eye
and we all stand beautiful before the sky
that sweeps around us and surrounds

each climber in a daze of open light.
Any way we turn, it's sixty miles
to farthest edge's curve, as flat earth falls
to the ball it is, thin-skinned, green, finite.

Must remind ourselves that this wide space
is in danger now, just as we are.
Poor would-be masters of earth, sea, air,
we belong to the mountain, not her to us,

or she belongs to all of us who ever
have climbed, or will, & burst out up here.

12

High up on the mountain's southern slope
a forest of tall old trees that has been dreaming
in sun & rain for years & years is being
bought & slashed to serve the greasy hopes

of three or four money'd little men
for firewood & space to build pink condos
& weekends for the rich. In oily lingo
they talk of sustainable development.

The vast clearing gapes, a raped corpse's sprawl.
Machines crawl over the ripped & opened hill.
They have their permits. What they can, they will.
Heads nod in the Ministry. Progress is all.

Hidden we watch from a torn edge green yet,
helpless in shadow: this is the way of the planet.

13

Tonight a consultation hearing on
bylaws proposed by a detested council
who will detest me too & wag their pencils
at my facts, at the evening wearing on

& at the mountain out there in the dark
they want to strip & gutter like a whore
& use & get off on & use till there's no more
& leave her grey in the rain, wash their work

away & with weekend cottages
cover her, cover her with lawns
& brokers' attractive children & keep her down
with pesticides, pave over her messages.

So I'll go tonight & say what I must say
& see their old eyes roll & wander away.

14 first meeting of the land trust

The meeting comes to order. Nominate
a secretary & a president.
The latter says it'll all be done in French.
The anglos hesitate & raise no hands.

Agenda is adopted. President
remarks. History, objectives &
founding members, grants & quest for finance
& what can be borrowed, what legally lent,

servitudes, in Quebec only
on adjacent properties, except
in cases of. What's given, what is kept.
But will this really work to save our only

mountain? Last, questions from the floor.
Answers drone. Is there one question more?

15

Attacks by vandals all around the mountain,
vicious invasions of deepest privacy,
sledgehammers & crowbars playing notes all crazy
on piano, chairs, the owners' beds of pain

or joy. What's the difference when opened
to those eyes' glassy hate in your absence?
Nothing personal, it's just that tavern sends
them & their buddies one dim idea: offend.

Why? because we can't be letting them
sell off the mountain in little tiny lots,
because it's no way to treat a mountain, not
this last one anyway. Our strategems

& traps are set: me, I don't answer
muffled calls. Shotgun's in the corner.

16

Meeting after meeting after meeting
& up there in the haze & in the sun
the mountain has its own agenda, season
& reasons for its high & green waiting.

We paw & crawl & climb the glaciers
of slow-moving paper documentation
for court case, referendum, consultation,
four years now among the sinecures

of stone politicians, unassailable
steep faces of the township councillors
jowl by jowl with developers
palisading deals at polished tables,

four years of sweating & clawing our way up.
What's a mountain? What's that mean, develop?

17

Nancy, Nancy, quite her own, comments
with her hands laid palms down softly on the table
& tills our complexity to grow as able
& flower in ideas as it was meant

to do & making sure we understand,
returns to listening. Pours the tea
sometimes, sometimes drifts to sleep when she
senses repeats or dither, wakes up when

the words push & pull & something decides
to change our view, all at once to act
along another tactic of attack.
Considers the dangers, sums up what we've said,

suggests we wait for better ground to fight,
then go for it. And she is usually right...

18

He calls me up at six o'clock to tell me
we're in the clear, the CPTAQ
did acknowledge our first letter. Whew.
Six AM we're talking. Up since three

with one of his beautiful ideas
of mountains & governments & the clerks in between
each with need to be seen or to be unseen,
the whole web glittering before his eyes-

so I take the cordless to a warm round chair
& yawn & listen & yawn then really listen
first to the clarity of his form, & then
because it's really happening out there

to the heart of the mountain both of us hear,
we discuss what we can do today for her.

19

Let me see now, April fourth is out
because of the court case, may go to the fifth
& if it goes for us, that will cut
the rest of April from the scheduled breadth

of days I've tried to set aside for poems,
the making them, their wu wei of arriving
of themselves, and now days I was saving
burst leaks & fill slowly up with deadlines

& meetings & if the council brings in by-laws
in late March, there'll be a referendum
after thirty days, so say May's a sure loss
except to glance at a green haze on the mountain

which is what started all this fuss & fun,
& it's Poems vs. Undeveloped Mountain. Mountain, one.

20

My god these politicians are ugly, ugly-
all image & inside a jumble of ignorance,
jowls clean shaven. Only their chins can dance,
their bodies blocked into chairs, luckily.

Gaia & her queens rule by gestures
known for truth & right by beautiful
economy, the hand giving when it's full
& when empty, giving emptiness for sure.

But these hands are knuckled in, design to take
& stuff the heavy corpulence below
& scratch a little the hanging dildo
as it twitches to erect, develop, invade.

Invade, control, put down the real dream
of high rock & pine, breathing in the solar stream.

21 gulf

What I don't get, she said, is how he can
pat the braids of that white-toothed little girl
in the street he descends into the whirl of
from his armoured staff car, his gun

hanging from huge khaki belted side
within a cluster of ducking bobbing fawning
local people, parents, friends, his great yawning
moustached power radiating wide

in the grainy video we watch, when he knows,
she said, voice breaking, that she's going to be,
all her small quick sweetness, all that she
sees & feels & dreams, dead & torn & stacked with rows

of other children. That's what I don't get.
What do you mean, he said. That's war. That's it.

22 office

A long afternoon of papers & reports.
Out the window, which is open still
a plane drones by. A few hundred kills
in the Gulf, the radio says, then Bach retorts

that this entanglement, too, is of the stars.
But now he is replaced by a thumping band
briskly celebrating death with life &
repeating heroes in a rosy glow of wars.

Now a waltz, the kind uniforms & long skirts
swoop & plunge in, and now thank god again
pure music, heuristic of the sense
we hope all this will make someday, in dirt

of ruins added to Mesopotamian dunes.
I sit back, face brick wall, empty of runes.

23

For some women sex is not an act
between friends; it's a hot zero of pain,
gone through under closed lids, sprawled under rain
& under night skies' blackness & it's just a fact.

A teenage girl I know was raped in a barn
by a hired hand against a dusty haystack.
Three years ago. Since then she's been racked
by a knowledge of that nothing nothing can burn

away, cuts her wrists & belly with razor
lightly enough to live, deep enough to show
her boyfriends. She doesn't know that I know.
Her wide fake smile, to me, is drawn by the closure

of her mother & father, turning away from her,
by the numbness she repeats, that now becomes her.

24

Cries of animals bellowing out their lives
& echoing back & forth between concrete
walls of zoos, cries in terrible heat,
cries of a woman being beaten alive

into a kitchen floor, cries of men
buried by bulldozers, amputated in tents,
herded & rooting like pigs behind a fence,
punched through with hot slugs, in gutters
leaking phlegm,

creaking calls of trees tilting & crashing,
cries of hungry babies left on the sand,
small cries in the buzz of flies around them drowned,
comic bubbling cries, cries of the falling.

I can't listen. Their cries can't be my cries.
What kind of song could I make of these?

25 for j.d.

Day by day nearer to the old ones,
you & me both, my longtime friend, my Jer,
here's some sloppy tangles for you to peer
severely at & jeer. If you've told me once

you've told me a thousand poems I didn't want
to listen to or live with their untidiness
of isolated feelings, their painful mess
of truths, dust bugs of poetic accident

swirling out grey nebular patterns from
the corners of our lifelong conversation,
dust poems from Ninevah, my true friend.
At last I concede that my life had turned from

the random suffering, the meaningless,
all love changing, its agony changeless.

26

We are the victims of the civil war
between the states & the conditions of being.
I scout my grey interior & I am seeing
the hate of you now, the love that was before,

the faithful widow'd mother raped to bleeding
her shame out on a hot & sunbaked street
as among carcasses of newborns maggots meet
in tangled ecstasies of heat & feeding.

Her boys have sodomized the enemy
& need our utter pain to calm their own,
to become the village stoning & the stones
gathered for this last group psychopathy.

No worry. No one left to see us die,
we'll swell to sausages under a cloudless sky.

27

Fall day, pale sunlight, hunters will come soon,
the crack & valley howl of their kills
will slam into our exercise of skills,
the quiet skills, my long & thinking runs.

Our cats have left half mice, a rag of bird
under the porch table, our glimpsed deer now
grey that were rich red, fresh dirt at burrow
entrances to fear, then sleep, in the code

of season. I draw a long releasing breath.
Flourescent jackets now. A spot between
shoulderblades itches, waking from tumbled dreams.
I think about the other side of death,

what the eye of the doe sees as she sags & crumples,
what winter is & leaves & always makes simple.

28

Good time to think about my guns & other
people's. The old carbine from Westerns needs
cleaning. My 94's sliding breech
sticks a touch, its slick click-music bothered

by a tiny bit of gum which I remove
with an oil rub to a sheen I can almost hear.
I ram a bolt action with a straightened wire
to clear a mud-wasp's nest. My eye moves

through the Special, flipped open so I might rage
at life from its brief & narrow helical tunnel,
but don't. I polish them all with oily flannel
& put them all away, put on my badge,

go out to check the hunters' licenses,
free of arms. This freedom whets my senses.

29 for sherman young

Up this morning, five o'clock & dark
first day of rifle season, have some breakfast,
pour tea in thermos, listen to the forecast,
then out to the car still only half awake.

Above the road grey sunrise gathers, stretches
out over the ridge across the valley's pool
of mist swirling amidst the claws of old
maples, reaching for light & what it touches.

Vans & pickups line the road I go.
I check their plates & stickers, call the base
to let the wardens know I am awake
& rolling & hearing what I need to know.

Knives pulled on us, barrels in the neck,
but it's people, it's the deer. So what the heck.

30

Took this morning off from wardening.
The roads are empty, the roads we ride along
looking into woods, field edges, for wrongs
within our jurisdiction. What's happening

out there beyond our view is another thing
altogether. Shots rip the misty air.
Mouths fill with blood, spirits die in fear.
The silence of woodpeckers follows the echoing.

Men's intention fills the trees with acrid fumes,
poison cordite mind surrounds the deer
& stops their breath & eats into their fur.
Through my window the shots are coming home

to my ear, at least. My tea turns cold & bitter.
It's time to suit up & get my ass on out there.

31

I didn't really know anymore if I cared
or if I did, what I cared about.
This morning Moki heard the bus & shouted
for me to run up the drive in the cold air

but my cough wouldn't let me follow her
so I called as loud as lungs would let me, wait!
She paused, divided, not wanting to be late,
not wanting to leave without the hug of father.

We met halfway. Don't worry, I said, he won't
go without you if he sees you coming.
She stretched up then from lunchbox, bookbag, warming
face in my shoulder's hollow a quick moment,

then doors swung open for her, left me at one
with my coughing, brilliant valley mist, the sun.

32

O so many afternoon explanations
of what truth is already in our bones.
The tea runs out & we run
out of everything but questions.

The snow along the track out there at noon
under the mountain is crosshatched & incised
with the pawprint lines of histories
purposed under the most recent moon.

I want to be there, but couldn't live
in the snow like that. Day comes
& on skis & clothed warmly, I come
to look, look into, look past self.

What is there to explain? Just heat up
the water, somebody. Here's my cup.

33

Whatever it was I was saying to whomever,
is all at once thick air around my tongue
as though I had been lying all along.
Down there you seem selfless as the weather

& luminous as earth, your wandering
a sudden stop to my intricate explaining
of the real current political situation,
a stop to my words as though they had never been.

I forget to whom I'm talking. The window bars
me from calling. I extricate from patter
with muddy promises of meetings later
in the week, & heading for the stairs

am too late, you're not there when I burst out.
The trees' arches are empty, though I shout.

34

So temporary, so temporary all this:
last night showered meteors Anna climbed
the peak to watch while I stayed home & rhymed
so I missed the whole celestial business

of brief hot burnings, lives, yes, like our lives,
you know the metaphor for some among us
whose love is wonderful yet never belongs
to anyone for long, from empty sleeves

is plucked & held aloft, then disappears
back into the mind of the magician
& leaves us standing in the empty rain
after the show, a memory of gesture

all that's left us, going home in dreams
& having to live through a yearning for all that seems.

35

As everything I used to want is old, or gone
& the new wants replacing them are needs, rather—
for bone-comfort, a simple place beside mind's fire
to soak in light as well as heat, as catch can

make do & eat a bit now & then
& remember when a want was real want,
tight shimmering in groin, tip a hot taunt,
the light play over the landscape of her skin

a startling pain to turn from, yearn back to,
& see fading back there where she came from,
pulling my banging heart down in whatever dim
her slight smile slightly bucktoothed turned back to,

disappearing into rainbow as though she was just
light receding, not the only want, maybe the last.

36

Last night I slept & dreamed of Liljan
standing on the dock my ship was leaving
& suddenly I was grieving, grieving, grieving
the thin cotton wind lifted, played again

soft up around her legs & over her small
Venus & upturned face I couldn't bear,
fearing the pain tangled in her long hair
as between us water widened to a grey wall,

an ocean between us. I never saw her again.
I never will except like this, awake
in the night, a dream bringing it all back,
all I refused to see & feel then,

her endured love, the faces & bodies since
not intervening in, worst, her warmth, her scent.

37

And what's she gotten from me? Her tobacco,
now a self-enclosing, not what the spirits
meant tobacco for. I still smoke for it,
the wise weakness, child I always go back to.

The sinuousities of Mingus on again,
I ride them in some smoky bar of haven
on the draw to her of my imagination
& the ashtray between us as it began.

My songs are sung to others. She doesn't hear them.
My love goes to my love & my son & daughters.
She has forgotten truth, & only fears her
consequences & hides because she fears them.

In the pull of smoke, I have to understand:
I gave her nothing & nothing's what she's found.

38

Today it may be sunny or it may rain.
In either case I want to find a poem.
I want it for you as a diadem
of love & pain & the pastness of that pain.

Your face, smiling & open at the window
I wave to & walk away from again & again
never & always for the very last time,
will never & always be there for me to lean to

as I leave, as I am always leaving
each day behind, pulled backward into time
by the whirlpool of your last pantomime
there back of the dingy glass of our misgivings,

me sealed & dumb in my wordiness,
you shut in your agony of unhappiness.

39

No matter what I say to you it's wrong:
either I'm trying to control you or
claiming who you were when who you are
is diverse & rarified as wind or song

or I have abandoned you when you
abandoned me. In the hate of a stony face
I see what others did. I pay their price,
though your truth projected is no longer true.

All I've wanted is to love you. Love you,
not make, fall in, be in, just do, not take
or want anything but talk, true talk. Of late
don't even want that, not even to save you

from your own angry denial, to help free
you from the self-same web too tangled round me.

40

I thought we were the flower poised above
the growing plant, the nearest to the light,
the oldest to the earth, the deepest root
to the mother of underground blind waters of love.

I am instead a ripped & gasping stem
twisted in your daisy chain of needs,
yanked into the sun & burnt in my seed,
one of your memories, like all of them

dying in what should have been the dawn,
what should have been moist silence of the earth,
& is what it is instead, a pretty death
& a shrivelling under the powers of the noon.

All woven into place, you crown your brow
with passions cut, to get their last high glow.

41

The difference between a girl & a woman
is the difference between the stars & earth
of gardens & vineyards & bearing & birth.
Your stars are a long way into never again

& stay that way, passions you don't believe in,
don't have to live with, only love
in the past where they belong & you get off
on one after another, weaving in among

their distant boiling energies not yours.
A woman comes into her secret own,
the past is her orchard & a sacred ground
for seeds of things to come her own hand pours.

No, I haven't made you a woman. No one
but the woman herself knows how that is done.

42

Looking at your face, it's nothing I ate,
nothing left of that old wanting pain,
no sleepless night in a bed of my own,
& I think hard, I think maybe it's too late.

I think maybe it's a pattern in our genes,
a special twist in the helix of our fate
that makes it time when it's time, so very late
when it's too late, & when we're in between

it makes us talk about the infinite
& find it in our eyes & mouths
& in our bodies' spiralling find truth,
& softly stretches us out into it

& leaves us, when the pattern's woven through,
in a smaller place, with smaller things to do.

43

I meet you once again in the Blue Café
quite unexpectedly & there you're sitting
across from me with all your fears fitting
around you, dark scarves, in your ear dry laughing.

You say you have to go, but then you don't
& linger to say over, you have to go
but stay with eyes focussed outside the window.
I know you know you don't know what you want

except it's elsewhere, in another time.
I ought to know better, my words are much too urgent
for this lost love game, their waves are surging
across your face, in their din your eyes dim.

Leaving your body, already you are gone.
I'm silent, losing you. In a sense, you've won.

44

I feel you only on occasion now,
only when I stop my doing of what
I do to fill the emptiness in that
silence of feeling, looking out my window.

The house wall's alive with hornets searching for
a way in, a way out of the coming winter,
but I've got nothing to search for, no way into
close warmth again. What's love's shelter for?

No longer can I easily summon up
the cloud of whispers filled with meaning then.
I've seen your glowing eyes since then turn stone.
The hanging man & death keep coming up.

Medusa, once you were at my quick of heart
& now can't touch me, even with your art.

45

What else is really in it for you, woman?
Considering you've torn apart your shepherd
already, ribcage open to hook beaked birds,
his ping-pong head bobbing in the foam &

now you're home again, already bored
with writing up report & rationale
to send off to yourself, marked Personal,
For My Eyes Only, empty, self-assured.

Meanwhile his round mouth's O fetches up on shore,
somewhere. A killdeer runs & stops & cocks
ear at the ragged bundle in the rocks
still singing wind's monodies of war

between the land & sea, & answers all
with the same old burden of its ancestors' calls.

46

Swinging down the avenue in his ice cream
summerweight seventy per cent
polyester suit, ducking the sun glint
from the endless oncoming sunglasses of his dream,

he is the flip side of a photograph,
blank white as sand shore under a washed-up shell,
not a trace on his face of the claws of his own hell,
his ponytail tight, his empty laugh

loose in the oiled holster of his dream.
Whatever he knows of absence & pain,
whoever he isn't & whatever he's done,
he swings down the avenue & seems

a mirage in desert light, a featureless
smile button in a world turned creatureless.

47

I write this line in fine & spidery hand
across a doorway to love not different
from fear of death & grin of innocent
skull & bones banging on a bed of sand.

We are the butt of a joke cooked up by time.
Every day crawls, crawls still slower
& we keep forgetting what it must be here for
or what the punchline is, if it's a punchline.

Sometimes I glimpse other lives, lifting
a cafeteria tray & eyes, making change,
coming from, going to. And now they range,
the old rake says, his bony toes sifting

sand or ashes, whichever. Here's the line:
Caution! Love. Keep inside the dotted rhyme.

48

On tiptoe when I'm pissing out the window
so's not to wet the weathered windowsill,
I could tumble like a yellow pinwheel
through brilliant sunshine into bush below,

at the golden end of my own trajectory
evaporating of a broken neck,
light dimming into green, in this bright break
losing the thread of our unending story.

I could just lie there, say nothing again
& someone else would have to pay the bills.
You all would go on living against your wills,
push your own sons & daughters to men & women,

fuss with adjustments to your aging plumbing
while I would lose myself in that bush's humming.

49 for the masters

Despite your handicaps you are whole men,
each craziness, each drug, each power to this
a door widening & deepening your bliss
turning love to want to pain to songs of pain.

Your eyes level with me as we meet.
You have been there where I'm going to slake
who knows what, a fire, a dripping beak,
warm oil, a disappearing act, a freak

only our imagination mates
with the spirit moving all of you as one,
the one I fear where you have feared & won.
My brothers gone before, through all mistakes,

you bodhisattvas, seedy saints to come,
in the hovels of your lives you host the sanctum.

50

Hands behind my head & daydreaming,
white clouds & butternut leaves are all I see
in morning sun, and those, brimfully.
No room in my eyes for any more seeming,

for any more season's yearning green of hope,
with this primaeval seeming of the leaves themselves
filling them, filling me with the leaves
themselves, though they'll wither in cold wind. Nope,

hope is for the birds flying north
in the spring. I'm in another season now.
The light is resting along each heavy bough
& all soaks in the heat, the length & breadth

of summer, though death's returning & I'll look to stars
again & die & be reborn & bear.

51

In the wake of a crashing thunderstorm,
you know the kind, not just around your ears
but through, completely through your brain aware
of each snap of waterdrop upon the tin

in downpour as particular & general
as sand, & as impersonal as fistful
flung in your wide-opened receiving eyeballs
or as the big-flaked snow clumping down your old

average winter night sky, landing wherever,
on glove, on hand, on cheek of one with whom
one spoke intensely under streetlamp light, when
one, whoever, with whomever, joined or severed,

noted flake on cheek. Now note the rain
in its true crashing, & take it as a sign.

52

Writing to find the sonnet's real way
before she ups & leaves me flat, flies home.
(That first line was for tomorrow's poem,
but now I'm in the tomorrow of yesterday.)

Would she leave me so? You bet she would.
Yet where is home for sonnets, in these days?
The sonnet which is more than private maze
or verbal seduction or pedestal of wood

painted to look like marble which in turn
was carved to look like what the past seemed then.
Tradition: patriarchs pat bums again,
stuff ashes of flashy passion into an urn.

The sonnet's more, or less, than such lost lace.
The man's poem. His pretensions, his grace.

53

The poem's always in interplay between
the form & tongue's gnarled daily surfaces,
iridescences & dark places,
the wells of speaking into which we lean.

Too much form, it's dead; too much nature,
it's not a sonnet. In that, like a woman,
half wild half friend, half vision half omen,
always at the edge of gift or capture.

Don't get me wrong. If ever you get her down
so she can't move, you've lost the real woman.
That's the worst. You'll have a specimen.
Same holds for poem: it never will belong

to you & you'll be asking who you were,
in your grip dead flesh of words & no answer.

54

Ho hum you say, sonnets on love & all that,
nothing new there, just the same old strings
of women, affairs, dreams, all distancing
endlessly, strings to jerk us about

& jerk us from & back at one another:
you turn me to puppet, I turn you
to oiled machine, & we do what we do
because we really aren't brother & sister.

Crazy cocks & cunts, yes, that's just it,
they trap us into dreams & in ideas
& in one another in all sweet ways,
but who can give them up? From where I write,

the sonnet's form is of our suffering,
yet blesses, heals, accepts our offering.

55

In the sheer writing now is sanctuary,
catch of breath, the place that heals wildness
of need. Grey cold day, my body's oldness
creaking with new truth, wiser & wary

of repeating faults past lives make easy
to me. I smoke a cigarette to bring
me into the invisible tunnel between
us, the dark concentric, our ecstasy

of time & place apart from one another.
Between us there are continents. Between
us, only this brief sinking into one
& stop to heart, at the edge of other.

I speak your name in there, over & over.
I write this more as you, than as your lover.

56

This morning Melissa tells me pain is a treasure
& I look out on rain & tumbling tree leaves
& Melissa tells me her fields are on fire with griefs
& I allow as how we live outside all measure,

really, that the wind is shouldering us
out into truest life, the sorrow we need,
the hollow secret hurt we hold & feed
against all order of mind, disordering us

now with a remembered touch of then,
laws & rules with the sledgehammer of this,
the robots with a gesture that just is—
or was, because she tells me how it's gone

& Melissa cries, come on let it rain,
so I do & fill with the weather of your pain.

57

Could you summon up the touch of my lips
in the long nights you were away from me?
My lips could, my tongue, my hands, my body
lying whole in your warm envelope

of touches, explorations all; could taste
you as you were when you were here & near
to this beating in my veins & fire
in head & groin & throat. Remember the last?

How not remember? There is no forgetting:
nights crazy with a grief I couldn't still,
couldn't share: that presence of the absent all
of you around me, your skin smell a letting

go the trance of pent tears each night:
it was true burning & a pure burning out.

58

Wake in the night with you an image in mind,
must be left over from a dream I had,
nothing left of, up in bed & mad
on empty content while outside the wind

claws at the roof to get in & mess me up
& weave into the strands of returning sleep
its own unrest. This is the void I keep
dreaming, the call always on my lips

come back, come back, the leaning backward into
space & darkness for those lost lost words
of synchrony & love. First chirps of birds,
no going back now: I lean beside the window

looking out on grey, still seeing you
about to say something healing and/or true.

59

Sleepless tossing nights, hot cold flashes.
Mornings, leaning out the study window
into brilliant sunshine flare of light, into
green & leafy elderberry bushes.

Would do the common thing, reach in the night
& my fingers would find only the empty bed.
This morning you were back, one thing led
to another world, our eyelashes tangled in light.

Love fills us up & empties us again
& again & we cry out to be filled all the time
but that's not the way it works. The holy rhythm
turns pain to ecstasy to deeper pain

to ecstasy more still than water can be,
to the pain of the night itself, hollow, empty.

60

When I think of everything you put me through,
the monkeyfaces & the pungent flowers,
the roar of sex-tides & tides of slow longing hours
when the empty bed beside me was empty of you,

your face turned away, your eyes burning in shadow,
your hands in dream touching Other's skin,
seeking ecstasy elsewhere, drawing it in
to yourself, all I think because you had to,

as I have had to; we each have our list,
& long, too. When I think of everything,
I wish we could do it again, each reaching,
each desecration, seeing how much we missed

going through it, even together, when we were,
swimming a sea of barbed & plastic lures.

61

Weavings from Charlie Mingus on the horns,
a warm breeze blowing through my studio
& in a wave of feeling how I loved you so
I remember how you turned & I was torn

wanting to think of you & wanting not to,
wanting to be with you & never wanting
to see you again but needing your sweet haunting
& wanting to die if I could live without you,

all clichéd lines from old & smoky songs
come home to me in whisper after whisper
& nothing's unique about these words on paper,
but over the wandering bass beat, what was wrong

between us is husky sweet & lost in the night
again, yet when it comes, is here & right.

62

Snapshots remind of the pool of rainy light
we swam in, that last long afternoon,
but because they only remind, give back none
of my life's wants. Was mostly there too late

or when I was there was not quite really there,
but once was different, so entered we were
into one another, one another's
luminousness & grace & fragrant air

that time was not, & it was not a time
to list with other times, good times, bad,
to file away with notes of what we've had,
but a glimpse we've had of what we were, the same

love that opened shutter in that room,
that knew it good & no good, but still presumed.

63

Quiet early April evening. The sky
has been robin's egg, the texture of your skin.
Cigarette. Again I sink within
to meet you, face floating in shadowy

waters of smoke drifting through archetypes
of change, hazards of pain of opening mind.
You were there, undulation in the wind
that today was still. I held a rising hope

twined as a double helix column of lovers
pausing on some street corner of wonder
to touch, breathe, enclose what all remember
of dark sweet need who saw them standing there

& passed by, having a place & time to go,
pain appointed. I release you so.

64

Nothing to say, I guess. Nothing to guess
at. Today so far I've emptied all
the wastebaskets, cleaned my desk, pulled wool
over my eyes about the emptiness.

Errands to do, things to buy, repair,
everything is as it was before you came
into vision again, but this time calm,
the jazz on the radio listens to desire

but knows none, intricacies of gossamer
float unattached patterns through this mind
which is still & dark as the waters of the pond
down there in the hollow of earth's ear.

Calm is good, I guess; at least it's free.
The sun just now came through & shone on me.

65

Wings stretch & dive toward me, banking to brush
my shocked face, an eye bright black & poised
through a fraction of a second's still release
of momentary meeting in a hot rush

of utter recognition. Love is like this.
For years we can live with someone, then at once
a look holds, burns in, a holy confluence
comes & is gone, leaves an ache of likeness

in empty air. My brother, my sister, my lover,
in our flash of looking we greet & grieve the other,
our lives & death rise to poise & are over.
We are left to carry this in all weathers

of cold heat, mere eating & sleep in mere air,
absence reminding how sheer love was, & there.

66

Saturn's day today & I am in
my Saturn's return, my dark mirror year.
They'll tell you it's something we must all endure
& nothing to fear but what is all your own

but this morning it's raining. The day, the day is dark
& I'm listening to the change in changeless rhythms
as to the grace & discord of my own strategems.
From outer space has come this special quark

plummeting from the edge of the speed of light
to penetrate my crown, my brain, my speech,
my heart, my gut, slowing when it reaches
the secrets & the nightmares & the dreams of flight.

I have been entered, as inlet by the sea,
as day by rain, by the woman already in me.

67

Felt against my stomach the bathtub's rim,
looked down. The sister of my mother smiled
& asked if I liked what I saw. My words failed:
Guess so, was all. She was so white in the foam

I couldn't look away, pretend I wasn't
looking, didn't see the naked goddess
under my nose. My open mouth confessed
wonder a boy of four years old just doesn't

have words or thoughts for, only holds forever
after, carries high in his double heart
through years of search through all his hungry art
to answer, to honour with words her stopped ears never

will hear: sister of my mother, you gave me
joy's vision to use, gently & wisely & gravely.

68

Up & out & yawning, scratching grizzle
& drinking tea & trying not to smoke
unless this sonnet goes for total broke
& its poem must be born & not just left to fizzle

so here I sit, hot tea digging cold sore,
noting down the present human condition
(at least it's tea & hot), still widdershins,
against the light, world against aching shoulder

& now taking the first drag of the morning
it drags me down into the sympathy
that gives a poem our blessed synchrony
& fills a passing moment with becoming.

Suddenly I think of you, waking
just about now & look: I'm all shaking.

69

A roar of wishes like the wind surrounds me
& carries me tumbling down over each day
so unlike each other, nobody
looking for me knows where to find me.

Leafing through all my jumbled images,
I try to hold to one, try to make one
but I am not the words she leans upon,
I am the acid wind itself that savages

her lilacs, trees she's planted through the years,
her lupines' soft spikes, her open wild roses
all tearing, flattening, dodging my unease's
caprice & force. Then suddenly her tears

stop & still me. I see what I have done,
all because I thought myself the wind.

70

I'm reading words from an old old notebook now,
all that rush of interleaved emotions
I see for what they were, just dumb illusions
that there was nowhere we had to go,

that we could hold by tongue touch all we had
in brilliant mornings, rainy afternoons
for a year or two. It happens, late or soon
& happened to us. Enough that we were glad

there & then, enough the long cold walks,
enough the selves we mirrored each to each
& what we grasped out past their farthest reach.
That time is gone & not gone & gone. Our talk

begins & from the wreckage of our tongues
owns up first to those touches when we were young.

71

The topic is always the same, always. Eros.
(You see how I've squeezed him to the selvedge
of poem if not of mind, to the living edge
itself. Themselves. Ourselves. One's self. Yours.)

My tongue traces the horizon on your lips
& you are you again, holy as unique
& tongue tells lips tiny ways to make
restings upon the surfaces of sleep

with you, the wash of tides between us ceaseless
on our waterbed, through years of nights
together as apart, the twist of sheets
rolling up some private dream of weasels

cornering & slashing in the night tunnels
& from fanged grins backing in, alone & funneled.

72

This conversation with a woman's shadow
goes on day after day in the deep of mind,
the blame in our voices floating, unassigned,
eyes disengaging, wandering to a window,

meeting branches & the mist in them
& nothing else. Nothing takes the place
of dreams, no opening of light in space
reveals echelons of seraphim,

& yet we talk. The vision you once were
may not return from all this nothingness,
I may have to live with shattered promises
of all we've fought & loved each other for.

But now you sit, facing me in human pain
like mine, healing. More than sane. Kind.

73

Except for what can never be satiated,
are you satiated now? Think we can talk?
About your crystals & your story-rocks?
About the way your sensitive nose is mated

to bloom & clump of moss, cupped in hand,
to skin of orange torn? About the way
your voice fits into the wind & what you say
has the sense of coming a long way over land?

Or how it lifts a strand of hair from temple
& kisses nape just here & here & here
& smooths skin, opening each drinking pore?
All these ways others reach you. So simple:

we'll never be satisfied, you by enough,
I that you love me only, more than life.

74

I open a window: frogs chunk from the pond
& below me mist is waiting for the sun,
as I wait for you to want me & to be drawn
into sleepy early warm awakened

need to draw me softly into you.
You snooze on. I go make coffee while
I wait. The grinder whines & water boils.
The stairs again, balancing your brew.

It's not my touch that wakes you, but the smell.
Out you come, your dream birds wheeling still
around you. With coffee & gratitude you fill.
The morning itself fills you, & you are full.

We joke & smile. Still wanting to be wanted
I dress & eat, drink tea & write this, haunted.

75

This morning was grey, this afternoon is grey
or many greys rather, infinitudes
of nuance, tone gradation, tint of mood-
differences inward is the country way.

Nothing much was happening this morning,
nothing much is happening today:
I'm not at all sure what I want to say-
you'll learn it all, if you are into learning

anyway. I can't change you, any
more than I can change the weather, you me,
your hair's magic randomness as truly
just here & tossing, one, among the many,

as the stillest miracle beyond my touch,
past wanting to change you into such & such.

76

The storm is moving on, out there in darkness
the lightning flashes are farther & farther away.
Thunder rolls to nothing. Nothing stays
but my astonishment, your likeness.

Out there in the night beyond my mind,
the red after-dazzle in my eyes
too wide to the night to bear your brilliant lies,
your slash of truth still comes & stuns & burns

but now its energy is moving on
& at my window here above the pond,
night sky clearing, my blindness almost gone,
hearing the frogs again begin their song,

I begin somehow, no, continue in
this voice that opened when I let you in.

77

You said when I first knew you, you wanted truth.
I'd lived so long without it, I just wanted you.
Then you wanted me within you too
yet now it's truth I want, more than breath

& yet the truth opens through you to me:
mist blue of heron on the shore, swallow's
freedom in its element, allow
as you allow. I am free as you are free.

I need you in your truth, you me in mine,
to understand you past your sweet treachery
& the wound of your deep-sunk hook of intimacy
& to understand my clinging & my whine,

each from each hole of our hiding. You drew me,
but now you move me & only the truth moves me.

78

Trying to keep faith when no one else here does
is bitter water to drink, it keeps you alive
but no one's there to want what you have to give
which is nothing to fuck or eat, nevertheless was

the gift of a star, dying out in space
yet shooting down its shining on your head:
breathe it in & look down from the dead
too soon returning to some star's hot grace.

A child's gift of pebbles & tangled grasses
her father doesn't know what to do with
but understands the giving's nothing to fool with.
Keeping faith, you meet such careful careful faces

yet always will hold out, without a price,
your gift unrecognized of earth & sky.

79

You want to know what days & nights were like?
An endless winding of useless sympathies
into a helpless circling of the world's needs,
into every blind yearning, each hot mistake,

& you a dream come true & not yet true
beheld fully only in my sleep
& I drew nothing I could own or keep
of all I'd lived for, all that I'd lived through.

Richness in that sleep, once I saw you.
It's true, every morning when I woke
I turned my face flat to the sky & spoke
through all that gossamer tangle how I knew you

from each illuminated grassblade, flower,
your presence in everything, everywhere.

80

There's a mirror you're always looking for
to know who it is you really really are
& a frame to hold & cold glass to bar
anyone else from coming in your door.

But the mirror-like wisdom's entered in my bones
& fountains from the gestures of my hands
as silver in sunlight arcs & rainbows & descends.
I'm not looking for mirrors, I am one.

When you are blue & open, I am the sky.
The need you pour out flows into my touch,
returns to graze & smooth the warm skin's stretch
of ecstasy we share along shared thighs,

not yours, not mine: the world's transparency
returning as open window to your eye.

81

In the middle of our twenty-year argument
we went to bed one night & there we found
nested in the pain circling round
the mouth I always meant, the breast you meant

though sometimes & in certain places & ways.
O there's a history all right.That's right,
& there's been a dim hole in my heart
where warm holding & milk in my early days

was by the stars denied, a tired old story.
And you, a girl become a sudden mother
still looking for the woman rising in her.
So what happened? Beneath all memory,

my mouth knew, you knew, below the tears & sex,
a first trance of suckling, the letting down your milk.

82

Hot, yesterday, today, in long rehearsal
down in a grassy bowl of shouldering hills.
A big sax just behind my right ear bawls
& my fingers ache & my notes jumble & spill.

My mouth's tight hurt against the embouchure
won't soften. Director keeps changing all the cues.
Long waits, long arguments, no rage let loose.
Do we repeat to B? Are you sure?

Nobody knows what's really happening.
Two weeks left & everything's a mess.
I haven't seen you. Where are you? Around, I guess.
Yet down through hot hues sinks the evening

as you roll & share a cigarette with me,
smile, & I know things'll be as they will be.

83

Left my lights on through both rehearsals,
of the Circus & the Band, so, my car dead,
stayed with V. all night in the pickup's bed,
dreaming storms of problems, knots of hassles

not lying on the side on which I snore
because she'd have no other bed to go to
& we're on this narrow futon feeling woe to
tired dancer's back & poet's more

than common need to sink in woman warmth.
But all night long my delicate fingers
laced the pearl of surfaces & contours
& cupped self to her vessel of breathing forms.

Even now I do, as I write. We woke afresh.
Car started, I'm home & fleshed in her radiant flesh.

84

Although I see it through this sometime veil
of pain, I see it as one beneath the many
shapes it changes into. Love's my meaning.
Because love is one, it's the changes I feel

in their flux, their coming & filling & failing & fading
& the winter silences when, underground,
love as the seed of all, wraps self around
& forgets who she is, until the maddening

begins in sleep, she dreams of something unfolding
& other, & then it all begins again,
a cycling through desire awakening,
excitement, climax, peace, talk, beholding

then surrendering name & form to the principle
between us in bed, a warm & pulsing jewel.

85

Sitting here in morning sunshine writing,
the Circus getting ready all around me,
the guys with job lists haven't found me
yet & still I keep last night's soft wanting

in my body, in my body still the ache
of entering delight & wetness in the dark
of you & such tremulous whispers lurk
& stutter with such lines no mind could take

beyond waking. The meaning of all this
escapes my pen & circles round the words
I almost find, almost piece like shards
together into the vessel holding peace

fashioned from that old old world of night
around our bones & buried from the light.

86

Your hair these days is cloth lightly woven
mostly black around your face, your eyes
dancing, deflecting, reflecting light of rise
& glow of set. Your hair is a medium,

an element to swim in & rise from to air,
from kissing nape, tugging at pearl lobe,
descending to circumnavigate each globe
& lower, into the wet forest of your other

drift of coastal salt weeds streaming with
each tide tonguing each inlet & beach
along your narrow straits, up to the reach
of ocean crashing wide around megaliths

of dreams, to the temples of your seven grey hairs.
Ah, you take me in again after all these years.

87

Late morning richness of remembering
your slim pearl length beside me breathing dawn,
your milk in my mouth, your mouth's wet searching down
my body's wakening, skin's shimmering

return to the light, return & rising arch
toward each other's need & wondering.
A red bird burns now under the rhododendron
canopy beside this sunny porch

quick in the corners of my eye & mind
& now is gone just as suddenly
as came & went this morning's symphony
of fire we find & lose, let go & find—

look: the cardinal's back. We cling in passing.
Our fingers lace again in each unlacing.

88

The undulating arch of your slow bending
is early light over me, your breast
hovering over my mouth, over my chest
your lips tasting, playing a neverending

game for the children we were & now become
again. Oh my woman, my only woman,
the silence around this breathing there is room in
for us alone, through us for everyone,

is a silence of sighs & tiny cries of joy
that after all this time together & apart,
we are together. Here meet nature & art:
thought moves your body now, thought moves my body.

This is what our dawn waking offers.
This is what we have to give to others.

89

Don't I wish. The living together in more
than peace, peace welling up inside of me
as tears do but not as tears of enmity
or of losing everything in continual war,

peace upon your lips & upon mine,
peace around their delicate strange meetings,
peace within their flights & deepest feedings
& every toast we make in homemade wine,

peace around the invited phallus, full peace
around each emerging child, each one wanted.
To each home, each stranger, each hunter & hunted
the gift of being held, the gift of release.

Don't I wish. But each outward journey starts here,
underfoot. Ours we share, & we'll go everywhere.

90

When I am a swallow in wind & light
banking & diving to meet & mate in air
over water, down off the mountain, sheer
as fall of stone from the sudden edge of night

you are all at once here, abrupt & wild
beside me in the buffeting of wind,
the double helix of the sharing mind
of flight itself between us, undefiled,

original dream of disentangling, free
from fear of death its power & from falling,
endlessly carrying on wings & in calling
back & forth across dreamt sky & sea

our reaching for whatever is constant in
love flying & grounding, over & over again.

91

My lovely friend, my heart, my thirst & light,
this late night thunderstorm is rolling off
& the frogs each sing their urgencies as love
pouring into the dark indefinite:

whoever's there to hear when I try to cry out
& answers my choked desire with desire,
whoever I am, whoever you are out there,
you're in here also, nameless still & right:

not knowing what I most wanted to find,
not knowing who, now it's you I've found
beside me in the night, shimmer of the pond
under a rising moon, a falling wind.

Out there others call as we have called.
My body cups to the shape of yours & holds.

92

I'm writing this poem with you in the room beside me.
Significant or what? It's always been
a secret process, I & this wavering line
from near one edge to near the other, it fights me

in the presence of another, but not today.
I would write freely anytime, I could
be in love with anyone over my shoulder, would
be the other side of you, if I had my way.

Today for some reason I do & the presence of you
is not the presence of another mind
or eye or body but what my other hands
are doing & what you are thinking is what I do

here in fragile script across the world
of the page from which this poem stirs & unfurls.

93

This form is a sort of paragraph, a way
of sorting, consulting, shaping into voice
my return from hunting hunters by choice,
the dark place of choice within, to say

what there is to say no one seems to be saying
in the cloud of conversations that surrounds me.
Simple as a Shaker chair, this form found me
aching in the field & straightens my wavering.

The gun stuck in Sherman's weathered neck,
the knife pulled on Claus & me on the road that night
I hereby draw within this frame of light
& shadow shading softly into black,

& so I'm back again & still alive
in the love I used to have, will have, & have.

94

What do I want? To be sheltered by the sky,
to be friends with the moon as it waxes & wanes
in your body's tides, its ecstasies & pains,
never to ask the coming winter why

you are here, have gone or have returned,
but just rejoice in what is past
as much as what is coming, first or last
of love as it soothes sustains renews & burns

everything away, away, again & again.
I want only your sense of time & space,
not to kiss so much as read your face,
in the act of love or just in conversation

for me a window out upon the stars,
their hieroglyphic above our nights & wars.

95

The eye enriches the more it is deprived.
In these darkened woods & fields the long greys
& browns of autumn slowly come alive,
away from colour screens & ad signs, away

from the sense-overload of the street's demands.
Here, the grey-brown flash of a running deer's coat
is flash enough, the eye's deepest command.
The buildings when we return from our long walk,

that once were brick-dull & weathered to grey earth
now stand in reds & browns before the mountain,
voluptuous as Maya, bathing to give birth
to the teaching child emergent, cascading, a fountain

of wealth to the seeing, food to the hungry sight,
gift of the halo, the habit of living in light.

96 visit

Drop the Toy into four-wheel drive & over
a steep rocky tractor road through dense
conifer hillside forest, without a glance
of the fitful sun through open cloud cover

ruffling the wide valley fields outside.
And here now is our violinist's clearing,
the cabin he raised his boys in, often staring
into the loneliness of his gifts, afraid

of nothing but not of the silence here.
He plays a seasoned knobby log for us
with maple sticks, interplay of forest's
form with chance with mind's finest ear.

Flute echoes trees. Talk, dandelion wine,
meal spare. True hearing. Goodbyes. No violin.

97

There are many messages in the wind,
especially this morning, the first flakes of snow
hissing warning to our slopes below
to descend like them, enter & be within.

And be like them, unique six-pointed stars
wheeling down from cold & cloudy birth
to cover & be covered & melt in warmth
returning. To them the end of winter

is the end of all. Like them we're surely not:
I hear their falling shush as a falling on,
white silences sealing me from the sun.
But the sharp sleet sings of Tristram & Launcelot,

whose flames burned against the truth of weather
& died of the cold we only survive together.

98

Just now Willy's gone to sacred ground,
a good neighbour's bright kid. Radiance.
Out that night under the stars of chance,
hit a tree just before the dawn

& vanished, rippling from his last dark drop
out to the edges of this edgeless pool
of sheer wonder at such life, at all,
his circle opening out to shadows, and stopped.

We have met in grief. Today, alone
with his call to live as though each waxing moon
cost such a death, such a boy, the beauty of him
gone into night & fire. Now's the pain

of the sudden falling away, having to give him.
Of our children's pain, the part of them gone with him.

99

That night massaged Luigi's ankle, sprained
by jumping too fervently from the Circus bus
in front of twenty thousand facing us,
& we talked of holy clowning & body pain,

& whether if ever we would meet again,
in Milano or Vermont, this life or next.
Taking leave, spoke of becoming correct
in our lives, in art, becoming men.

In our goodbye embrace he called me *bello,*
just that word, casual but meant
so I took it, tongue-tied, for something sent,
& carry it with me now, gift of a fellow.

Driving home, thought: we must be everywhere,
& the planet needs us, scattered, near & far.

100

Love is not a thing but a dimension
that present makes all things possible,
makes living possible, makes us capable
of passing through this time/space emotion.

It isn't what we do for or with, but to
each other, chokes me up & makes me open
to death & want the seventh seal broken
open & sky to open her final blue,

to let us take one open breath of air,
just air, just stop & look at one another,
not as father mother lover sister brother
but as aspects of mind so infinitely fair

we'd love each other as we ought to love
ourselves, our self, which is all we really have.